BLAZERS

TOP 10
UNEXPLAINED

TOP 10
UFO and
Alien Mysteries

by Lori Polydoros

Content Consultant:
Dr. Andrew Nichols
Director of the
American Institute of Parapsychology
Gainesville, Florida

Reading Consultant:
Barbara J. Fox
Reading Specialist
Professor Emeritus
North Carolina State University

CAPSTONE PRESS
a capstone imprint

Blazers is published by Capstone Press,
1710 Roe Crest Drive, North Mankato, Minnesota 56003.
www.capstonepub.com

Books published by Capstone Press are manufactured with paper
containing at least 10 percent post-consumer waste.

Library of Congress Cataloging-in-Publication Data
Polydoros, Lori, 1968–
    Top 10 UFO and alien mysteries / by Lori Polydoros.
    p. cm. — (Blazers. top 10 unexplained)
    Includes bibliographical references and index.
    Summary: "Describes reports of various UFO abductions, encounters, and sightings"—
Provided by publisher.
    ISBN 978-1-4296-7639-7 (library binding)
    1. Unidentified flying objects—Sightings and encounters—Juvenile literature. 2. Human-
alien encounters—Juvenile literature. I. Title. II. Title: Top ten UFO and alien mysteries.
TL789.2.P65 2012
001.942—dc23   2011034689

Editorial Credits
Mandy Robbins, editor; Veronica Correia, designer; Eric Gohl, media researcher;
    Laura Manthe, production specialist

Photo Credits
Fortean Picture Library, 17
Getty Images/Aaron Foster, 28–29; AFP, 11; AFP/Joshua Roberts, 27
iStockphoto/Ipson-blue, 15
Mary Evans Picture Library, 9, 21; Michael Buhler, 7, 13, 19, 23, 25
Shutterstock/Alperium, cover (front), 5; Bruce Rolff, cover (background);
IND. photoBeard, 26

Printed in the United States of America in North Mankato, Minnesota.
122012   007098R

TABLE OF CONTENTS

Unidentified!... 4

10 Gulf Breeze Sightings. 6

9 Flying Saucers 8

8 Saucers in Europe. 10

7 Man Goes Missing! 12

6 The Phoenix Lights. 14

5 Lights in the Forest 16

4 Lights over Belgium 18

3 Foo Fighters. 20

2 Star Maps and Aliens 22

1 Strange Crash in Roswell. 24

Glossary 30

Read More 31

Internet Sites 31

Index 32

UNIDENTIFIED!

All through history, humans have spotted UFOs. People once thought UFOs were signs from the gods. Today some people think they are alien spaceships. Check out today's top 10 UFO and alien mysteries!

UFO—unidentified flying object

10

GULF BREEZE SIGHTINGS

In 1987 and 1988, hundreds of people in Gulf Breeze, Florida, saw UFOs. Ed Walters took photos of one of the flying objects. His photos were printed in the newspaper. Many people thought Ed's photos were a **hoax**.

hoax—a trick to make people believe something that is not true

FACT Walters also said he was lifted up by a beam of light coming from the UFO he photographed.

FLYING SAUCERS

In 1947 pilot Kenneth Arnold was flying in Washington state. He spotted nine objects flying near him. Arnold said the objects moved like saucers skipping across water. He made the term "flying saucer" popular.

SAUCERS IN EUROPE

Pilot and astronaut Gordon Cooper saw many flying saucers in Europe in 1951. Cooper said that these crafts flew higher and faster than his jet. U.S. military leaders thought Cooper saw secret aircraft from the Soviet Union.

FACT In the 1980s, Cooper urged the United Nations to officially investigate UFOs. They refused.

MAN GOES MISSING!

In 1975 a group of Arizona men spotted a UFO. A light beam from the UFO hit Travis Walton. The other men left in fear. Walton was missing for five days. When he was found, he said aliens had **abducted** him.

abduct–to kidnap or take someone against his or her will

THE PHOENIX LIGHTS

In 1997 a group of lights seemed to float over Phoenix, Arizona. Some people thought the lights formed one large UFO. Thousands of people saw the lights. The government said it was a group of military **flares**. But most **witnesses** didn't believe the government.

flare—a burst of light shot from a gun
witness—a person who has seen or heard something

FACT Former Arizona governor
Fife Symington thought the
Phoenix Lights were a spaceship.

LIGHTS IN THE FOREST

10 9 8 7 6 5 4 3 2 1

In 1980 military police in Rendlesham Forest, England, reported a UFO with colorful lights. Witnesses said the UFO left landing marks and burned treetops in the forest. **Skeptics** blamed the sighting on lights from a nearby lighthouse or a **meteor**.

skeptic–a person who questions things that other people believe
meteor–a piece of rock or dust that enters the Earth's atmosphere, causing a streak of light in the sky

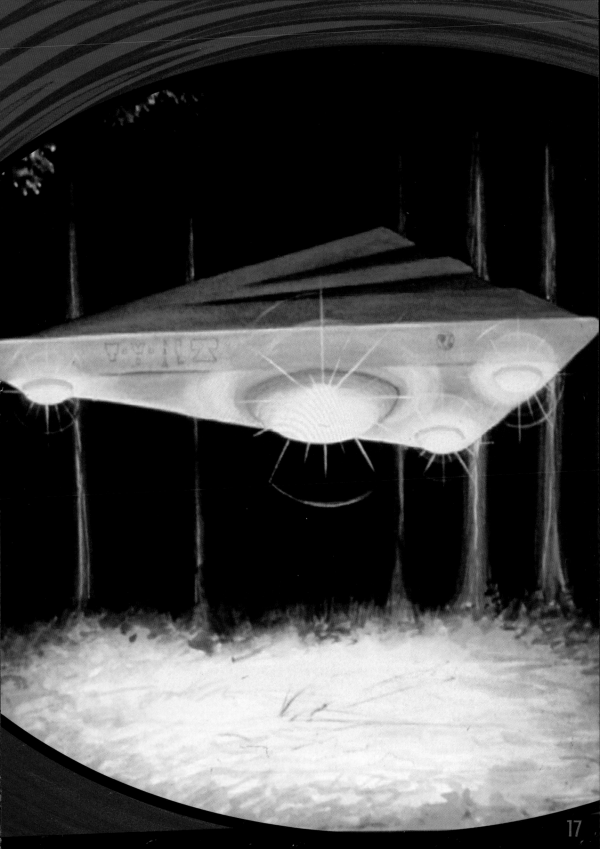

LIGHTS OVER BELGIUM

Between 1989 and 1990, thousands of people in Belgium reported triangle-shaped UFOs. The Belgian Air Force tracked one of these objects on **radar**. They could not explain its quick movements.

radar—a device that uses radio waves to track the location of objects

FACT A UFO wave happens when multiple UFO sightings occur over a period of time.

FOO FIGHTERS

During World War II (1939–1945), pilots reported glowing blobs floating in the sky. The pilots called them "foo fighters." Pilots from each side of the war thought they were the enemy's secret weapons.

FACT Some U.S. pilots flew at the foo fighters, but the lights would disappear.

STAR MAPS AND ALIENS

10 9 8 7 6 5 4 3 2 1

In 1961 Betty and Barney Hill were driving down a dark New Hampshire road. Suddenly, something strange happened. The Hills said they were taken aboard an alien spaceship. Betty said the aliens showed her a star map that showed their home in space.

FACT

In 1969 a researcher matched up the Hills' star map to a star system called Zeta Reticuli.

STRANGE CRASH IN ROSWELL

One stormy night in 1947, something crashed near Roswell, New Mexico. A rancher found the **wreckage** the next day. The military studied the crushed metal and sent out a **press release**. A flying saucer had crashed!

wreckage–the broken remains of an aircraft or ship that has crashed
press release–an official statement released to the media by an organization

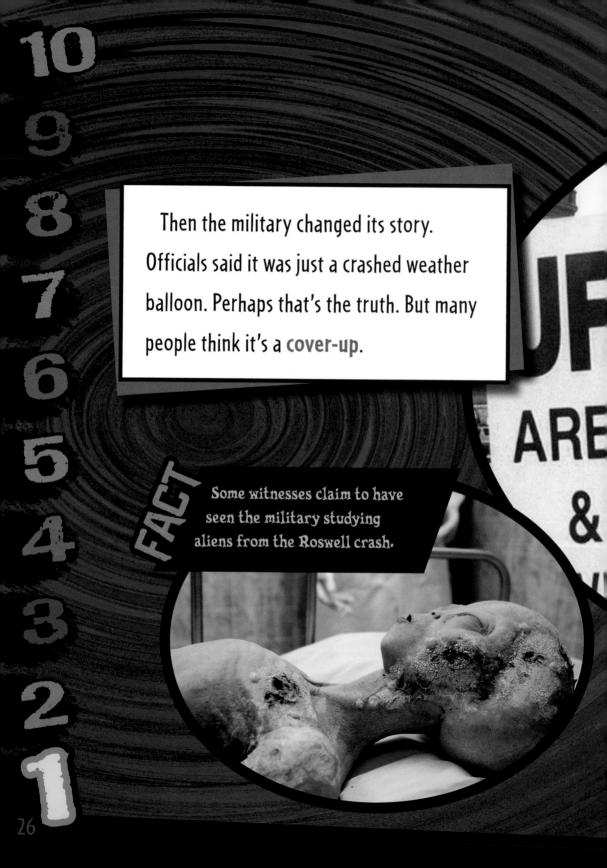

Then the military changed its story. Officials said it was just a crashed weather balloon. Perhaps that's the truth. But many people think it's a **cover-up**.

FACT Some witnesses claim to have seen the military studying aliens from the Roswell crash.

cover-up–an attempt to hide information

LOOKING FOR THE TRUTH

People all over the world try to solve UFO mysteries. Researchers talk to witnesses and study evidence. Maybe one day we'll learn the truth behind some of these UFO mysteries.

Glossary

abduct (ab-DUKT)—to kidnap or take someone against his or her will

cover-up (CUV-uhr-UP)—an attempt to hide information

flare (FLAYR)—a burst of light shot from a gun

hoax (HOHKS)—a trick to make people believe something that is not true

meteor (MEE-tee-ur)—a piece of rock or dust that enters the Earth's atmosphere, causing a streak of light in the sky

press release (PRESS RIH-leese)—an official statement released to the press by an organization

radar (RAY-dar)—a device that uses radio waves to track the location of objects

skeptic (SKEP-tik)—a person who questions things that other people believe

UFO—an unidentified flying object; some people believe UFOs are spaceships from other planets

witness (WIT-niss)—a person who has seen or heard something

wreckage (REK-ij)—the broken remains of a plane or ship that has crashed

Read More

Grace, N. B. *UFO Mysteries.* Boys Rock! Chanhassen, Minn.: Child's World, 2007.

Hawkins, John. *Aliens and UFOs.* Mystery Hunters. New York : PowerKids Press, 2012.

Nobleman, Marc Tyler. *Aliens and UFOs.* Atomic. Chicago: Raintree, 2007.

Internet Sites

FactHound offers a safe, fun way to find Internet sites related to this book. All of the sites on FactHound have been researched by our staff.

Here's all you do:

Visit *www.facthound.com*

Type in this code: 9781429676397

Super-cool stuff!

Check out projects, games and lots more at
www.capstonekids.com

Index

abductions, 7, 12, 22
aliens, 4, 12, 22, 26
Arnold, Kenneth, 8

Belgium, 18

Cooper, Gordon, 10

flying saucers, 8, 10
foo fighters, 20

Gulf Breeze sightings, 6, 7

Hill, Betty and Barney, 22
hoaxes, 6

Phoenix Lights, 14, 15

radar, 18
Rendelsham Forest, 16
Roswell, 24, 26

star maps, 22
Symington, Fife, 15

UFO waves, 19
United Nations, 10

Walters, Ed, 6, 7
Walton, Travis, 12
World War II, 20

Zeta Reticuli, 22